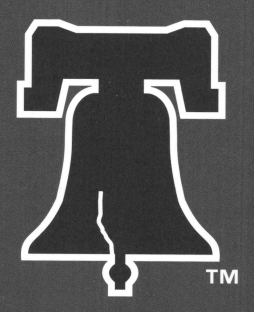

™

Hello, Phillie Phanatic™!

Aimee Aryal

Illustrated by M. De Angel with D. Moore

MASCOT BOOKS®

www.mascotbooks.com

It was a beautiful day for baseball
in Philadelphia. Ready for fun, the
Phillie Phanatic arrived at the
ballpark for a *Phillies* game.

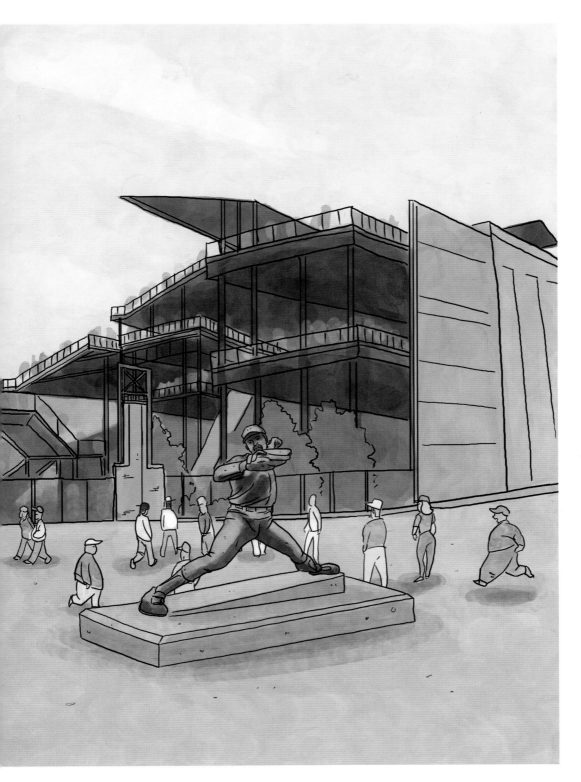

The Phanatic was greeted by a family of
Phillies fans near the Steve Carlton statue.
The family said, "Hello, Phillie Phanatic!"

The Phanatic made his way to the statues honoring Mike Schmidt, Robin Roberts, and Richie Ashburn. Seeing these statues, the Phanatic felt proud to be part of the *Philadelphia Phillies* family.

The Phanatic ran into two of his biggest fans and he gave them a special Phanatic hug. Everywhere the Phanatic went, Phillies fans waved and cheered, "Hello, Phillie Phanatic!"

The Phanatic arrived on the field in
time for batting practice. The Phillies
wore their red batting practice jerseys
as they took practice swings.

The Phanatic gave a Phillies player a
few helpful batting tips. The player then hit
several balls out of the ballpark. The player
said, "Thank you, Phillie Phanatic!"

After batting practice, the ballpark grounds crew went to work. With great pride, they quickly prepared the field for play.

One man wheeled away the batting cage,
while another man raked the infield.
As the grounds crew worked, they cheered,
"Hello, Phillie Phanatic!"

With the start of the game only moments
away, the Phanatic was feeling hungry.
He grabbed some snacks and a Phillies
pennant at the concession stand.

As he made his way back to the field, he ran into another family. The family waved and cheered, "Hello, Phillie Phanatic!"

As Phillies fans settled into their seats, the public address announcer introduced the Philadelphia Phillies. The loudest cheer was received by the Phanatic!

The team stood on the first base line,
removed their caps, gazed at the American
flag, and sang the National Anthem.
Afterwards, everyone cheered, "Go, Phillies!"

The umpire yelled, "PLAY BALL!"
and the first batter stepped to the
plate. It was time for the first pitch.

The Phillies pitcher delivered a perfect
fastball. "STRIKE ONE!" called the umpire.
The game was underway!

The Phanatic made his way into the stands to visit with some of his friends. He came across yet another family of Phillies fans.

His silly antics made everyone laugh.
Fans nearby cheered,
"Hello, Phillie Phanatic!"

It was now time for the seventh
inning stretch and the singing of
Take Me Out To The Ballgame!™

Fans sang arm-in-arm as the Phanatic led
the crowd from atop the Phillies dugout.
Afterwards, fans cheered,
"Hello, Phillie Phanatic!"

The Phillies trailed by one run in the
bottom of the ninth inning. With a
runner on first base, the team's best
player stepped to the plate.

With a powerful swing, the batter launched a home run! A lucky fan caught the ball as it landed in the bleachers. The crowd cheered, "Phillies win! Phillies win!"

After the game, Philadelphia Phillies fans
celebrated the thrilling victory. The Phanatic
left the ballpark and headed for home.

The Phanatic crawled into bed and fell fast asleep. Good night, Phillie Phanatic!

For Maya and Anna. ~ Aimee Aryal

For Sue, Ana Milagros, and Angel Miguel. ~ Miguel De Angel

For more information about our products,
please visit us online at www.mascotbooks.com.

Copyright © 2007, Mascot Books, Inc. All rights reserved.
No part of this book may be reproduced by any means.

Mascot Books, Inc. - P.O. Box 220157, Chantilly, VA 20153-0157

Major League Baseball trademarks and copyrights are used
with permission of Major League Baseball Properties, Inc.

ISBN: 978-1-932888-85-0
PRT0610C
Printed in the United States.
www.mascotbooks.com

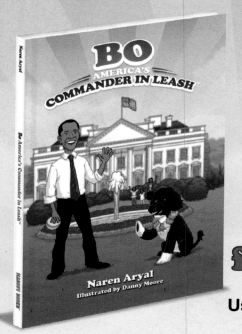

America's most
famous mascot, Bo!

Use promo code *bo* to receive *free shipping!*

Baseball

Team	Title	Author
Boston Red Sox	Hello, *Wally*!	Jerry Remy
Boston Red Sox	*Wally The Green Monster* And His Journey Through *Red Sox Nation*!	Jerry Remy
Boston Red Sox	Coast to Coast with *Wally The Green Monster*	Jerry Remy
Boston Red Sox	A Season with *Wally The Green Monster*	Jerry Remy
Boston Red Sox	*Wally' The Green Monster And His* World Tour	Jerry Remy
Chicago Cubs	Let's Go, *Cubs*!	Aimee Aryal
Chicago White Sox	Let's Go, *White Sox*!	Aimee Aryal
Colorado Rockies	Hello, *Dinger*!	Aimee Aryal
Detroit Tigers	Hello, *Paws*!	Aimee Aryal
LA Angels	Let's Go, *Angels*!	Aimee Aryal
LA Dodgers	Let's Go, *Dodgers*!	Aimee Aryal
Milwaukee Brewers	Hello, *Bernie Brewer*!	Aimee Aryal
New York Yankees	Let's Go, *Yankees*!	Yogi Berra
New York Yankees	*Yankees* Town	Aimee Aryal
New York Mets	Hello, *Mr. Met*!	Rusty Staub
New York Mets	*Mr. Met* and his Journey Through the Big Apple	Aimee Aryal
Oakland Athletics	Let's Go, *A's*!	Aimee Aryal
Philadelphia Phillies	Hello, *Phillie Phanatic*!	Aimee Aryal
Cleveland Indians	Hello, *Slider*!	Bob Feller
San Francisco Giants	Go, *Giants*, Go!	Aimee Aryal
Seattle Mariners	Hello, *Mariner Moose*!	Aimee Aryal
St. Louis Cardinals	Hello, *Fredbird*!	Ozzie Smith
Washington Nationals	Hello, *Screech*!	Aimee Aryal

Pro Football

Team	Title	Author
Carolina Panthers	Let's Go, Panthers!	Aimee Aryal
Chicago Bears	Let's Go, Bears!	Aimee Aryal
Dallas Cowboys	How 'Bout Them Cowboys!	Aimee Aryal
Green Bay Packers	Go, Pack, Go!	Aimee Aryal
Kansas City Chiefs	Let's Go, Chiefs!	Aimee Aryal
Minnesota Vikings	Let's Go, Vikings!	Aimee Aryal
New York Giants	Let's Go, Giants!	Aimee Aryal
New York Jets	J-E-T-S! Jets, Jets, Jets!	Aimee Aryal
New England Patriots	Let's Go, Patriots!	Aimee Aryal
Pittsburg Steelers	Here We Go, Steelers!	Aimee Aryal
Seattle Seahawks	Let's Go, Seahawks!	Aimee Aryal

Basketball

Team	Title	Author
Dallas Mavericks	Let's Go, Mavs!	Mark Cuban
Boston Celtics	Let's Go, Celtics!	Aimee Aryal

Other

	Title	Author
National	Bo America's Commander In Leash	Naren Aryal
Kentucky Derby	White Diamond Runs For The Roses	Aimee Aryal
Marine Corps Marathon	Run, Miles, Run!	Aimee Aryal

College

School	Title	Author
Akron	Hello, Zippy	Jeremy Butler
Alabama	Hello, Big Al!	Aimee Aryal
Alabama	Roll Tide!	Ken Stabler
Alabama	Big Al's Journey Through the Yellowhammer State	Aimee Aryal
Arizona	Hello, Wilbur!	Lute Olson
Arizona State	Hello, Sparky!	Aimee Aryal
Arkansas	Hello, Big Red!	Aimee Aryal
Arkansas	Big Red's Journey Through the Razorback State	Aimee Aryal
Auburn	Hello, Aubie!	Aimee Aryal
Auburn	War Eagle!	Pat Dye
Auburn	Aubie's Journey Through the Yellowhammer State	Aimee Aryal
Boston College	Hello, Baldwin!	Aimee Aryal
Brigham Young	Hello, Cosmo!	LaVell Edwards
Cal - Berkeley	Hello, Oski!	Aimee Aryal
Cincinnati	Hello, Bearcat!	Mick Cronin
Clemson	Hello, Tiger!	Aimee Aryal
Clemson	Tiger's Journey Through the Palmetto State	Aimee Aryal
Colorado	Hello, Ralphie!	Aimee Aryal
Connecticut	Hello, Jonathan!	Aimee Aryal
Duke	Hello, Blue Devil!	Aimee Aryal
Florida	Hello, Albert!	Aimee Aryal
Florida	Albert's Journey Through the Sunshine State	Aimee Aryal
Florida State	Let's Go, 'Noles!	Aimee Aryal
Georgia	Hello, Hairy Dawg!	Aimee Aryal
Georgia	How 'Bout Them Dawgs!	Vince Dooley
Georgia	Hairy Dawg's Journey Through the Peach State	Vince Dooley
Georgia Tech	Hello, Buzz!	Aimee Aryal
Gonzaga	Spike, The Gonzaga Bulldog	Mike Pringle
Illinois	Let's Go, Illini!	Aimee Aryal
Indiana	Let's Go, Hoosiers!	Aimee Aryal
Iowa	Hello, Herky!	Aimee Aryal
Iowa State	Hello, Cy!	Amy DeLashmutt
James Madison	Hello, Duke Dog!	Aimee Aryal
Kansas	Hello, Big Jay!	Aimee Aryal
Kansas State	Hello, Willie!	Dan Walter
Kansas State	Willie the Wildcat's Journey Through the Sunflower State	Dan Walter
Kentucky	Hello, Wildcat!	Aimee Aryal
LSU	Hello, Mike!	Aimee Aryal
LSU	Mike's Journey Through the Bayou State	Aimee Aryal
Maryland	Hello, Testudo!	Aimee Aryal
Michigan	Let's Go, Blue!	Aimee Aryal
Michigan State	Hello, Sparty!	Aimee Aryal
Michigan State	Sparty's Journey Through Michigan	Aimee Aryal
Middle Tennessee	Hello, Lightning!	Aimee Aryal
Minnesota	Hello, Goldy!	Aimee Aryal
Mississippi	Hello, Colonel Rebel!	Aimee Aryal
Mississippi State	Hello, Bully!	Aimee Aryal
Missouri	Hello, Truman!	Todd Donoho
Missouri	Hello, Truman! Show Me Missouri!	Todd Donoho
Nebraska	Hello, Herbie Husker!	Aimee Aryal
North Carolina	Hello, Rameses!	Aimee Aryal
North Carolina	Rameses' Journey Through the Tar Heel State	Aimee Aryal
North Carolina St.	Hello, Mr. Wuf!	Aimee Aryal
North Carolina St.	Mr. Wuf's Journey Through North Carolina	Aimee Aryal
Northern Arizona	Hello, Louie!	Jeanette Baker
Notre Dame	Let's Go, Irish!	Aimee Aryal
Ohio State	Hello, Brutus!	Aimee Aryal
Ohio State	Brutus' Journey	Aimee Aryal
Oakland	Hello, Grizz!	Dawn Aubry
Oklahoma	Let's Go, Sooners!	Aimee Aryal
Oklahoma State	Hello, Pistol Pete!	Aimee Aryal
Oregon	Go Ducks!	Aimee Aryal
Oregon State	Hello, Benny the Beaver!	Aimee Aryal
Penn State	Hello, Nittany Lion!	Aimee Aryal
Penn State	We Are Penn State!	Joe Paterno
Purdue	Hello, Purdue Pete!	Aimee Aryal
Rutgers	Hello, Scarlet Knight!	Aimee Aryal
South Carolina	Hello, Cocky!	Aimee Aryal
South Carolina	Cocky's Journey Through the Palmetto State	Aimee Aryal
So. California	Hello, Tommy Trojan!	Aimee Aryal
Syracuse	Hello, Otto!	Aimee Aryal
Tennessee	Hello, Smokey!	Aimee Aryal
Tennessee	Smokey's Journey Through the Volunteer State	Aimee Aryal
Texas	Hello, Hook 'Em!	Aimee Aryal
Texas	Hook 'Em's Journey Through the Lone Star State	Aimee Aryal
Texas A & M	Howdy, Reveille!	Aimee Aryal
Texas A & M	Reveille's Journey Through the Lone Star State	Aimee Aryal
Texas Tech	Hello, Masked Rider!	Aimee Aryal
UCLA	Hello, Joe Bruin!	Aimee Aryal
Virginia	Hello, CavMan!	Aimee Aryal
Virginia Tech	Hello, Hokie Bird!	Aimee Aryal
Virginia Tech	Yea, It's Hokie Game Day!	Frank Beamer
Virginia Tech	Hokie Bird's Journey Through Virginia	Aimee Aryal
Wake Forest	Hello, Demon Deacon!	Aimee Aryal
Washington	Hello, Harry the Husky!	Aimee Aryal
Washington State	Hello, Butch!	Aimee Aryal
West Virginia	Hello, Mountaineer!	Aimee Aryal
West Virginia	The Mountaineer's Journey Through West Virginia	Leslie H. Haning
Wisconsin	Hello, Bucky!	Aimee Aryal
Wisconsin	Bucky's Journey Through the Badger State	Aimee Aryal

Order online at **mascotbooks.com** using promo code " **free**" to receive **FREE SHIPPING**!

More great titles coming soon!

info@mascotbooks.com